FOR JOHNNY

Poems of World War Two

FOR JOHNNY

Poems of World War Two
by

John Pudney

SHEPHEARD-WALWYN
LONDON

First published 1957 in
'Collected Poems'

This Revised Edition published 1976
by Shepheard-Walwyn (Publishers) Ltd, London

A proportion of the royalties from all sales of this edition
is being donated by the author to the RAF Benevolent
Fund

ISBN 0 85683 031 3   Hardback
ISBN 0 85683 029 1   Softback

Printed in England by
Biddles Ltd, Guildford

Contents

Foreword

The twelve lines of 'For Johnny' were first written on the back of an envelope in London during an air raid alert in 1941. I was, I imagine, on forty-eight hours leave from RAF Coastal Command Station at St. Eval, Cornwall, where I was at that time an Intelligence Officer. There and earlier on Fighter Stations during the Battle of Britain I had come face to face with the deaths of men younger than myself – to have just turned thirty was to be a very old man among the squadrons. Some of these losses were very close. Bitterly sudden too, between lunch and tea, half way through an argument or a game, in the midst of lovely country and in those years in the domestic setting of England. The experience was repeated far and wide overseas.

There never was a particular Johnny. The twelve lines which forced themselves on me virtually intact in one go, were meant for them all. It is the same with the named individuals in other poems: the one stands for many. Just as men went through a sort of de-identification before taking-off on operations, (required by security to empty their pockets of all personalia) so my verses sometimes re-identified mere numbers as familiar names. To this day readers continue to identify Johnny and the others with their dear ones, loved ones, acquaintances, comrades or boon companions. This is fair enough. A significant part of the nature of poetry is identification and participation.

I had worked for the *News Chronicle* before the war and from Cornwall I sent a typescript of 'For Johnny' which the newspaper published. It was signed J.P. because it was considered at the time that a serving officer writing under his own name on a 'Service matter' – and surely Johnny was that – would be a breach of regulations.

One really stirring result of its publication was a letter from

7

C. J. Greenwood of the Bodley Head saying that he assumed the poem was my work and that he would be willing to publish a volume containing this and others. 'Just send a selection and I'm sure we shall go right ahead . . . ' There were others: and in 1942 a volume called *Dispersal Point* was published, and was reprinted.

Soon after publication Stephen Potter, then in his pre-Gamesmanship days, devised a BBC programme of 'For Johnny' and the other poems with Laurence Olivier, then a Naval Officer, as principal speaker. Rehearsal and transmission took place during an alert but that was not the only crisis. The final line of 'Combat Report', a sort of reportage-ballad, went:

That's how the poor sod died.

A warning came somewhere high up that the BBC, even in the throes of war, would not permit the word *sod*. What about *soul*? Make it 'how the poor soul died'? There was a walkout and while the bombs crumped somewhere in Greater London the first broadcast of Johnny hung in the balance in an Oxford Street studio.

Eventually arguments based on poetic licence won and Olivier duly recited Johnny and for the first time used the word sod on the hitherto untainted air of the BBC.

I left Johnny in its slim volume, wrote some more, of which some appear here, and was sent on duty to Africa, the Middle East, Malta, North and South America and eventually into Europe. I was asked to broadcast Johnny in New York and in Cairo and that seemed to me the last I should hear of it and its companions.

Then came the making of the film *The Way to The Stars* directed by Anthony Asquith, scripted by Terence Rattigan. A request for the use of 'For Johnny' and 'Missing' came through the film division of Air Ministry and I was given some leave to visit the Shepherds Bush studios with some vague notion of helping with the presentation of the poems. Here I did little except to salute extras dressed up as Group Captains, and to suggest, without modesty, that 'For Johnny' should be spoken *twice* – a reprise being at the end of the film so that the customers took it home, so to speak. It was a contractual curiosity in that the company bought the film rights in the two poems – the first time, we all thought, that film rights in poems had been an issue.

The poems were spoken by Michael Redgrave and by John Mills: and through their talents reached, and from time to time continue to reach in revival, a public not normally tolerant of contemporary verse.

'For Johnny' lived on into my middle and old age with some persistence. Strangers quote it at me at unexpected moments – a commissionaire opening a door, a garage receptionist with tears in her eyes, a North Sea trawlerman, a girl in the Embassy in Athens. A truck driver said he and his wife recited it together 'to feel cosy'. It appeared without my knowledge in the *Oxford Book of Quotations*. It has been used three times on gravestones. The last six lines of it were found on the body of a burnt pilot – could I supply the first half. Raymond Blackburn quoted it in the House of Commons in a debate on Housing.

I feel proud, humble and battered in turn: for it all belongs to another life, a generation ago and too many well-meaning people expect one to go on writing the same thing over and over again for the rest of one's time.

My poetic life has been a football match. The war poems were in the first half. Then an interval of ten years. Then another go of poetry from 1967 to the present time of writing. The second half, for better or worse, is for me unconcerned and unaligned with the first. I am not writing in the context of a generation ago but for and about Now.

Meanwhile 'For Johnny' with the other poems has been for some years out of print, though in increasing demand, perhaps from another generation to whom the Hitler war has a period appeal and its air forces a nostalgic glamour reflected luridly in toys and models. So this new edition is offered to the grateful memory of old friends and with a contribution to a charity that still serves their memory, the RAF Benevolent Fund.

Greenwich 1976   JOHN PUDNEY

(O WAR IS WHISPERING)

O war is whispering in the barley,
And green ears sweeten in the sun.
O with charlock and red poppy
Weed-proud summer is begun.

Summer too innocent in beauty
Strips the eye which wakes ashamed:
Drenching daylight with high lark-song
Where the very sky is aimed.

In a chastity of air, war ventures,
Where the rose forms innocently whole.
In the ardent pallor of the barley,
War sighs, fumbling for the soul.

DISPERSAL POINT

I did not trust myself to know your names;
Nor dare to let you touch my coward heart.
I overheard the others call you James,
That you were good at games,
That you were in it from the start.

Apart you fly. You, with a surgeon's glance,
Grave and discriminate, enforce the dreams
Of mathematic theory. You advance,
From probable extremes,
To take a human chance.

A girl with laughing lips can make you cry;
You have been saving money for a car;
You never tell your mother where you fly:
Keeping your station in the sky:
Solitary cunning star.

Apostolic name, no hero, fellow
Mother's son whose secret is life only.
This is the coward's heart which does not know
How to laugh and let you go,
How to answer you, the lonely.

WHEN TRANQUIL HOURS SHALL COME

When tranquil hours shall come as sure as leaf,
And only love shall spoil the heart's good ease,
When weariness has drained the guilt and grief,
When, sure as winter, death falls; think of these,
These young and easy of heart, the single
Of hand and skilful ones who seek not death
In livid hours where past and future mingle,
Where live men petrify and dead catch breath.
The victim gods in an heroic age,
These ride like thunder where man's fear and greed
Are frontiers interlocked in mean outrage;
These fly, now engined by all human need.
These, wishing life, must range the falling sky,
Whom an heroic moment calls to die.

WE DO NOT SAY GOOD-BYE

We do not say good-bye:
We play no game of hearts:
Eyes too often lie.
Let's play darts.

Easier to nod:
We don't say what we think:
And, not being God,
Let's have a drink.

Easier, without friends,
Without the secret game,
Nothing starts or ends.
What's your name?

EMPTY YOUR POCKETS

Empty your pockets, Tom, Dick and Harry,
Strip your identity; leave it behind.
Lawyer, garage-hand, grocer, don't tarry
With your own country, your own kind.

Leave all your letters. Suburb and township,
Green fen and grocery, slip-way and bay,
Hot-spring and prairie, smoke stack and coal tip,
Leave in our keeping while you're away.

Tom, Dick and Harry, plain names and numbers,
Pilot, observer, and gunner depart.
Their personal litter only encumbers
Somebody's head, somebody's heart.

SO I PRAISE THESE

Do not suppose
The amazing daffodil has thrust
From the waste plot
Or the polluted dust.

Nor was the soil
From which a gallantry of roses flowered,
Luckless, unhusbanded,
By God or mankind soured.

So I praise these,
The gallant, the amazing, who from chance
Of birth or circumstance
This darker hour enhance.

In praising them
I celebrate a soil which is still sweet
In mine and mill,
In meadow and in street.

WHEN BULLETS PROVE

In times when bullets prove, when deeds decide:
Nor the cool laughter of the youthful corn
Nor brief hot poppies hide
Earth trodden and torn.

In times when smiling eyes and lips tell lies,
And only dead men tell no tales, no tales
Casting their last disguise,
Love alone avails.

Hold hard to the dear thought. For courage less
This tenderness is but a dress worn thin
Against the cold. Love's dress
Is blood-deep under the skin.

A SINGER LESS

One sang in the evening
Before the light was gone:
And the earth was lush with plenty
Where the sun shone.

The sound in the twilight
Went: and the earth all thin
Leans to a wind of winter,
The sun gone in:

One song the less to sing
And a singer less
Who sleeps all in the lush of plenty
And summer dress.

FOR JOHNNY

Do not despair
For Johnny-head-in-air;
He sleeps as sound
As Johnny under ground.

Fetch out no shroud
For Johnny-in-the-cloud;
And keep your tears
For him in after years.

Better by far
For Johnny-the-bright-star,
To keep your head,
And see his children fed.

SOONER OR LATER

Sooner or later, loss
And, cruellest of all winds, pity
Must blow across
My nature and my body's old resolve.

How shall I meet the blast,
The standstill of passion, winter
Of loss ice-fast:
And blood still blood that trims the will to live?

For better or for worse,
In laughter, in anger join me
When that adverse
Wind come.

I value this the most:
Companions with no more to lose,
That thrifty host
Which storms the barren times to live one hour.

Sooner or later, yet
Most lonely in all men, pity
Must still be met
Alone, perhaps in tatters at high noon.

COMBAT REPORT

Just then I saw this one come out.
You heard my shout? You, light and easy,
Carving the daylight. *I was breezy*
When I saw that one. O wonder,
Pattern of stress, of nerve poise, flyer,
Overtaking time. *He came out under*
Nine-tenths cloud, but I was higher.
Did Michael Angelo aspire,
Painting the laughing cumulus, to ride
The majesty of air. *He was a trier,*
I'll give this Jerry that. So you convert
Ultimate sky to air speed, drift, and cover:
Sure with the tricky tools of God and lover.
I let him have a sharp four-second squirt,
Closing to fifty yards. He went on fire.
Your deadly petals painted, you exert
A simple stature. Man-high, without pride,
You pick your way through heaven and the dirt.
He burnt out in the air: that's how the poor sod died.

NIGHT FIGHTER PATROL

Hereditary gestures, through the bone
Of rigid time and timeless flesh, derive
Likeness more final than the graven stone,
Likeness that is alive.

Now, in the cockpit, smile or flick your wrist,
Study the compass, glance across the main
Of tideless night. In such features exist
The fortunes of your strain.

The sailor's son or shop-bred boy or one
Whose people farmed hard acres share the style,
The faithful glance, the lively skeleton
Scaling the steep night with a smile.

SMITH

Smith, living on air,
Your astral body
A mechanic wonder,
Your anger an affair
Of fire and thunder.

Smith, who puts down fear,
Whose young heart
Grapples with pity, whose spirit
Holds life on earth so dear,
And death no merit.

MISSING

Less said the better.
The bill unpaid, the dead letter,
No roses at the end   .
Of Smith, my friend.

Last words don't matter,
And there are none to flatter.
Words will not fill the post
Of Smith, the ghost.

For Smith, our brother,
Only son of loving mother,
The ocean lifted, stirred,
Leaving no word.

ONE COUNTRY-BRED

Did Smith so love this land:
May love of country still
Cradle the fretted heart
With wold and hill?

May Smith, one country-bred,
Have set a meadow round
The near horizons of
High sky and ground?

Did Smith still live to kill,
Recalling trees in bloom
And, entering into shade,
Smile at his doom?

So did Smith love this land,
So love of country will
Enforce a heart-weak hand
And ease the iron skill.

CORPORAL ALICE

Corporal Alice dances like aspen:
And life is long
As the life of a leaf.
Corporal Alice chooses not often:
And not from love
Shall she come to grief.

Now all you sweethearts whisper with Alice
And all you wives
Smile close in the dance.
Somebody's mother answers with Alice:
And lucky lives
Are blessed by her glance.

Corporal Alice dances off duty:
And life is brief
As the life of the flowers.
Corporal Alice shall keep her beauty
Longer than leaf
Than war's lost hours.

NO SUMMER NOW

O frost fell early
Upon the flowering bough.
There is no summer now.

It is a story
As old as any they tell
How, still as death, frost fell.

How life was lovely
As life was never before
And will be never more.

Though season surely
Follows the season now spent
And fills man with content.

O frost falls early,
Old as time is the sorrow
Killed or cured tomorrow.

ROSES AND RUINS

Once more the rose, rally of English heart,
Blooms at the crater, at the ruined sill,
Where life left off, where love was left, where part
Of you or you stay still.

There is no public wrong or private grief
Can stain the colours, steal the proud design.
Autumn may snatch the petal and the leaf.
Now, the whole flower is yours and mine.

Lucky to live and greet the rose full blown,
Which blooms on death and flaunts the frightened hour;
To see the emblem of most inner bone
Clothed in the frail flesh of the flower.

WESTERN DESERT

Winds carve this land
And velvet whorls of sand
Annul footprint and grave
Of lover, fool, and knave.
Briefly the vetches bloom
In the blind desert room
When humble, bright, and brave
Met common doom.

Their gear and shift
Smother in soft sand-drift,
Less perishable, less
Soon in rottenness.
Their war-spent tools of trade
In the huge space parade:
And, with this last distress,
All scores are paid.

And who will see,
In such last anarchy
Of loveless lapse and loss
Which the blind sands now gloss,
The common heart which meant
Such good in its intent;
Such noble common dross
Suddenly spent.

GRAVES: EL ALAMEIN

Live and let live.
No matter how it ended,
These lose and, under the sky,
Lie friended.

For foes forgive,
No matter how they hated,
By life so sold and by
Death mated.

HAPPY-GO-LUCKY

Happy-go-lucky he
Heeded well
How shone the sun
The day he fell.

No man his debtor, none
Heir to this
Bloom no woman raised
To earthly bliss.

Happy-go-lucky he
Gave but heed
To laughter and that kiss
Which children need.

After the death spelt out in headlines, after the gains
Broadcast by the dispassionate voices,
Comes word to a village.
Loss with the lifted latch. With poor remains
Of the meal unfinished comes pillage
And ruin upon the country hearts of some.
The small death come,
And poor the sorrow shared by a few.

Not along with the old people beneath the yew
Lying at peace, not with those old
Comfortable ones sharing God's acre of ground,
Will he snore snug down under grass
For the idle and the children to cause and pass,
Hearing the enviable sound
Of the wind in the yew,
The wind in the yew.

Tom Roding, tractor driver, of Slare
In the County of Essex, son of the dew
And misted hedgerows, minder of riddies,
Comrade of the autumnal hare
Tawny upon the stubble. Lost to these widest skies,
Clodhopper, clay-built, your still eyes
Finding no final meadow, lost one,
One of the casualties, old George Roding's son.

News is written in blood and the radio words
Entering a cottage parlour are charged with lives.
Over Eazle Wood homes evening with the homing birds:
And summer listens to the gaffers and to the old wives.
No doubt there will be some village memorial.
There will be names cut for all to recall.
And the few who knew Tom Roding will fall
To their few regrets at evening, with the chill of the dew
And the wind in the yew,
The wind in the yew.

So was one life spent, of many,
In a mouthful of sand in desert in the bare
Vengeful enemy sunlight. For Jenny,
For Alice, for Flo with evening sound
Of homing birds is heart-loss, sorrow. At Slare
Come settle the sum of Tom Roding, tractor driver, heir
To widest sky, corn-ripple, harvest dew,
His saved wealth fifteen pound.
And O the wind in the yew,
The wind in the yew.

SONG OF THE CHANCES OF WAR

O ringing glass
And drowning sailor.
Some go to war
With words on paper.
O whistled tune
And luckless airman.
Some go to war
Sheathed in a sermon.

Some are too wise
To think it over
Or grudge to lose
Sweet life, sweet lover.
And lucky ones
Of simple stature
Kill not to kill
But serve the future.

O ringing glass
O luckless whistle.
The weeds grow proud,
Day crowns the thistle.
Ill-luck and lack
Go sickle-handed.
Keen is the blade,
The eye most candid.

CONVOY JOB

Convoy the dead:
Those humble men who drown,
Dreaming of narrow streets, of alleys snug
In lamplight, love in a furrowed bed,
Pints in a Rose and Crown.

Escort the brave
Whose hearts, unsatisfied
With the kind stairs and tender hearths of love,
Are loyal to the cunning of the wave,
The sparse rule of the tide.

Fly over these,
Humble and brave, who sail
And trim the ships with very life; whose lives
Delineate the seas.
Patrol their deathless trail.

AT SEA

My sheets are warm tonight
Though Love must lie alone.
My sheets are warm and white:
And Love is not a stone,
Not cold and adamant,
Not to sink in the sea.
While blood is vigilant
Lies Love awake in me:
As wide as the sour swell
That menaces the soul,
As danger tolls the bell,
As fear's sunk steeples toll.
My love, warm well my bed
While war frets out in storm.
For Love, wide in this head,
Keep my sheets warm.

WHEN ORDERS ARE TO LIVE

If men with lives to lose have any luck
The bell will toll for them another day.
Lucky are they who hear this hour struck,
Impatient while the minutes slip away
To lean again upon the roomy air,
With brief regrets, but loving life the more
And lovelier for life. Who shall prepare
An order of the day which shall restore
The finer temper to the man, to break
Bright generous sun upon the human frame,
Choosing not whom it fire or whom it wake
By whispering to each timid soul by name?
Pray God shall raise such honour and such skill
When orders are to live and not to kill.

AIR GUNNER

The eye behind this gun made peace
With a boy's eye which doubted, trembled.
Guileless in the mocking light
Of frontiers where death assembled.

Peace was as single as the dawn,
Flew straightly as the birds migrating,
Timelessly in tune with time,
Purposeful, uncalculating.

So boyish doubt was put away:
The man's eye and the boy's were one.
Mockery and death retreat
Before the eye behind this gun.

THE BLIND

To be alive like Sam,
Sam balancing his beer
Upon his chin:
Sam somersaulting past the chandelier,
Performing his flat spin.

To be alone like Sam
Would be to watch the place
Of Ropey Jack,
To miss the concord of that bastard's face
Who isn't coming back.

SHORT LEAVE

With sudden ease,
And Mozart played at night,
Lamplight upon brushed hair,
Wind leaf-lost in the trees,
I am aware
How man must pay with love.

With little spent
And life to pay away,
Today, tomorrow, all
Are lost in the event:
And we are small,
All we who pay with love!

THE HEAD'S SECRET

No peace in the ruin.
No comfort in the dead.
Life lapsing in the body
Lives but in the head.

But seek you the last answer,
The final gout of grief:
This head replies with silence
Of an old belief.

No sign in bomb's dead litter,
No marvel in the sky:
But the head's secret only
Refuses to die.

REVENGE

Who said revenge?
The blind eye at the sights;
Lips, bloodied, crushed;
The old who pray at nights;
The white child hushed?

Whose vengeance proves?
Graves, nameless, innocent;
God on our side;
The hapless dead content;
And no more pride?

The eye that killed,
Lips that desired the kiss,
The young and old
Were innocent in this.
Revenge is cold.

You shall have your revenge who flew and died,
Spending your daylight before day began.
You shall have good hours back: and go in pride
Against the dark. Protagonist of man,
Account shall be for lives in measured days.
You shall inherit hours which are replaced,
The earth won back, the trustier human ways
From history recovered, on them based
An amplitude of noble life. Prelude
Shall there be none: nor count of other cost
Of dying, living, loving. O intrude
Your lively innocent ghosts upon the frost
Of present winter, quickening in its dearth.
Your vengeance shall be spring within the earth.

FALL

The tale of war, the story,
Same as rain, falls evenly on all:
And the words for honour and glory
Wear too small.
Too slight the words, and spoken
Too often, as sky and sight shake down,
The serene marble broken,
The stray shot killing child or clown.

Now autumn without pity
Burnishes all flesh and has no shame.
Lovers in wheat-field and in city
Make their claim.
O same as rain or seasons,
Falling, falling on lovers and all,
War falls, wastrel of rhyme and reason.
Honour and glory wear so small.

MAN ALIVE

Enough of death!
It looms too large in words:
And those who die
Know but the death of birds.

Enjoy the sky,
Possess the field of air,
Cloud be your step,
The west wind be your stair.

This province range,
Familiar of the sun.
The birds' strict life
Demands your stricter one.

Under your eye
The easy tits await
Hand pressure cool,
The wrist dispassionate.

But man alive,
By no horizon bound,
Unfenced, unroofed,
Roots hold fast in the ground.

MEMORIAL

For those who leave no trace,
Their heirs these times:
For those unlovely heroes:

For those whose fingers fall
On iron for love,
On weariness for pillows:

For those whose laughter went
Out with the light
In any evening's danger:

For young and old who die
At every hour
Now life is sole and solemn monument.

AT THE CEREMONY

One without orders came,
Deaf to the cheers,
His number up, his name
Lost in the years.

Within the lost years lost,
Under the banners,
A digit in the cost
Of the planners,

Comely and limber he
Marched in the host
Of the victors. Jauntily
Filled his last post.

COMMEMORATIONS

Commemorations and names,
As we grow old,
With our dates for battles and for dames
Have all been told.

In between the death of friends
Our story went
Endlessly outspun, to make amends
For what was spent.

Endlessly a solemn tale
Of glory runs,
From the men who had the world for sale
To their sold sons.